San Francisco

San Francisco

0-938440-08-X

Photos by: *Robert Glander*

Peter Gridley

Sandor Balatoni

Marino Bros.

Dennis Hallinan

Contents

This beautiful reflection enhances the magic San Francisco's skyline.

San Francisco —

Two unique San Francisco institutions:
Cable Car and Flower Stand

The Golden City

San Francisco is a young city, with all the pride and zest of youth. Because of the gold rush years, it developed quickly, uncontrollably, forced by its topography to grow upward rather than outward.

San Francisco has a mind of its own. It is fiercely independent, and enjoys being different from the rest of the world. It is protective of its colorful reputation. For colorful it has been, this unique city tucked in a pocket of the mountain-fringed West Coast.

It is also an impossible city. The terrain of the hilly peninsula on which it rests makes it an unlikely place on which to found a city. Still, there it thrives, a jewel glinting from the Northern California coastline.

It is a city of mystery, cloaked by the intruding seafog during the summer months. And in the winter, the inland fog gently brushes the hills on its way to the Pacific. But there have been moments when Nature dealt harshly with it, too.

San Francisco is also a brash city, charging into new ideas with little thought to consequence. But out of such brashness has evolved an amazing tolerance. Where else could Bohemians and Flower Children find a refuge as willing to embrace them as does this city? These young people eventually become new patterns in the everchanging mosaic that is San Francisco.

The city covers 49 square miles. Its altitude varies from sea level to 938 feet above. The Bay is the most important harbor on the West Coast. Commercially, San Francisco serves extensive areas of the West and Northwest. Nature helps to make it an active city. The temperature averages in the mid-60s, except for September and October when it may climb to the 70s. The mornings and evenings are a bit damp due to the famous San Francisco fog, but by the time the sun completes its ascent, the days are sunny.

The city's population is both cosmopolitan and provincial. This results from the diversity of ethnic groups inhabiting San Francisco. And each group, while cooperatively proud of its adopted city, holds and guards its original language and customs.

San Francisco attracts people from all over the world. While its history of family harmony has not been without blemish, foreign nationals tend to feel more welcome here than in most American cities. The international mix includes Chinese, Japanese, Samoans, Filipinos, Pakistanis, Greeks, Hungarians, Czechs, Yugoslavs, Russians, Jews, Irish, Welsh, English, Finns, Poles, Scandinavians, Blacks, Maltese, Italians, French, Germans, Portuguese, Spanish, Mexicans and other Latin Americans, American Indians, and the unmatched San Francisco Bohemians. Without a passport, one can visit several ''countries'' within the perimeter of this metropolis.

Above all, this is a city for those who enjoy life. The spirit of San Francisco is still adventurous. The people of San Francisco are buoyant, and they make their city buoyant.

This is the city blessed by the sun. This is the bay that took ages to form and centuries to be found. This is the strait carved by inland waters on their determined way to the sea. And it was all brought together by some fortunate destiny, creating a city with a crown of hills and with a bridge for its emblem, and it became The City by the Golden Gate—San Francisco

Above: The Conservatory of Flowers

Below: The M. H. de Young Memorial Museum, both located in Golden Gate Park

Overleaf: The City, Old and New

Right: Mission San Francisco de Asis, founded in 1776, popularly known as Mission Dolores

Left: Fisherman's wharf

Left, below: Candlestick Park, Home of the San Francisco Giants and the San Francisco 49ers.
Photo courtesy of San Francisco Giants.

Top: Alcatraz Island

Below: Aerial view of the city with Pier 39 in the foreground

Overleaf: The Golden Gate Bridge. The Bridge seems to float above the fog.

Below: Oakland Bay Bridge seen from the air

Night view of Oakland Bay Bridge.

Favorite Landmarks

All major cities have landmarks, but San Francisco is rich in landmarks that are found *only* in San Francisco. Here, bridges are not merely links between two points but also contribute to the city's personality. Islands are rich in history as well as being functional. The city builders have used to advantage the forbidding hilly terrain. The parks are an integral part of the city's life. And when one hears a reference to cable cars or flower vendors or Nob Hill, one thinks of no other city but San Francisco.

The Bridges

San Francisco has not one but two great bridges. At the time Joseph B. Strauss designed it, the Golden Gate Bridge was described as "the bridge that couldn't be built." Not only was the bridge built but it also became the city's most famous landmark, tantamount to a logo for San Francisco. But because of the treacherous tides and unpredictable winds, the rocks and the inevitable fog, the 1.7 mile bridge took over four years to complete. The eventual construction cost was $35,000,000.

The Golden Gate Bridge connects the northwestern tip of the Presidio Military Reservation with Marin County across the strait to the north. It is truly an engineering marvel. Its red-painted towers brace one of the longest center spans in the world, 4,200 feet. The two cables supporting the span 250 feet above the swirling tides are each made of more than 2,500 strands. When the bridge is struck by the setting sun, it resembles a harp of blazing gold. This beautiful structure was opened to traffic in May 1937.

Six months earlier, in November 1936, the San Francisco-Oakland Bay Bridge was put into service. This 8¼ mile bridge across San Francisco Bay is a two-level structure. At night, it is a striking sight with its strings of yellow sodium vapor lights whose rays are strong enough to penetrate the densest fog. This bridge cost $77,200,000 to build. From San Francisco, it crosses the Bay to Yerba Buena Island, crosses the island through a tunnel, then continues over the water to Oakland. It is one of the longest steel bridges in the world.

As well as being beautiful as objects of engineering, art, and daring, these two bridges make it possible for San Francisco to serve as central trade point for the West and Northwest.

The Islands

Alcatraz is Spanish for pelican, and the Spaniards named the island for the numerous pelicans that sought it out as their seasonal haven. Alcatraz Island lies about 1½ miles off Fisherman's Wharf and was once the site of a lighthouse—the first one erected on the western coast of America. When Alcatraz was turned into a Federal Prison, it acquired the nickname "The Rock" because it is indeed composed of solid rock. In 1963, all prisoners were removed from the 12-acre island, and Alcatraz is now a tourist attraction.

About a square mile in size, Angel Island is the largest island in San Francisco Bay. It is triangular in shape and has been an Indian prison, a military installation, an immigrant quarantine station, a military overseas staging area, a Nike missile base, and a dueling site in the earlier wild days of the city. In the 1960s, it was converted to a state park, and today more than 200 deer still rove freely through the trails of this island highly favored by picnickers.

Yerba Buena Island, named after the wild, profusely-growing mint that the Spaniards found there, is the anchorage of the two spans of the San Francisco-Oakland Bay Bridge. Connected to Yerba Buena Island is a flat, man-made island, Treasure Island, which was created to be the site of the "Golden Gate International Exposition" held in 1939. Today, both islands are naval installations.

Overleaf: San Francisco Bay and the Golden Gate Bridge.

Overleaf: Oakland-Bay Bridge with
San Francisco skyline in background

Right: Golden Gate Bridge wit
San Francisco in background

San Francisco's financial district, with
the Ferry Building tower in the foregroun

Out in the Pacific waters, some 30 miles west of San Francisco, are seven small islands formed out of rock. These are the Farellon Islands, rookeries for several species of sea birds, overburdened with rabbits, and visited by sea lions. These islands became part of San Francisco in 1872, and in 1909 the islands were designated a Federal bird sanctuary. On one of the islands, a lighthouse rises 358 feet above the sea and can be seen 26 miles away.

The Hills

Before it is anything else, San Francisco is its hills. This "impossible" landscape is responsible for the adoption of that popular mode of public transportation—the cable car. The hills also provide breathtaking views of the city and its environs, day or night.

The most noteworthy of the city's twenty-one hills are Telegraph Hill (300 feet above sea level) on which is built the famous Coit Tower, Russian Hill whose slopes were once the burial place of Russian seamen and is the site of Lombard Street known as "the crookedest street in the world," and Nob Hill where the former rivaling mansions and palaces of millionaires have surrendered to skyscraper hotels and apartment complexes. Twin Peaks, the geographical center of the city, is composed of two hills of equal height; it offers perhaps the best view of the city and the Bay.

The Parks

In 1871, designer William Hammond Hall turned more than 1,000 acres of wasteland into the largest man-made park in the world—Golden Gate Park. Wide lawns, flower beds, and small lakes provide places for dozens of recreational activities. The park is host to the California Academy of Sciences with its Morrison Planetarium and Steinhart Aquarium, the Conservatory of Flowers, the Strybing Arboretum and Botanical Gardens, the popular Japanese Tea Garden, the M. H. de Young Memorial Museum and the Asian Art Museum, Kezar Stadium, the Polo Field, and the Music Concourse where weekend concerts are presented.

West of Fisherman's Wharf is Aquatic Park which includes the Maritime Museum and the Maritime Historic Park. Stretching westward is Marina Park, the site of Yacht Harbor, and the Palace of Fine Arts with its new Exploratorium of science, technology, and human perception. Next comes the Presidio Military Reservation. Farther west, Lincoln Park is the site of the Palace of the Legion of Honor and of the Veterans Administration Hospital. Along the Pacific shore is Ocean Beach, reaching from Cliff House and Seal Rocks south to the Zoological Gardens and the Lake Merced-Harding Park recreation area. In the southeast corner of the city is McLaren Park just north of the famous Cow Palace.

In addition, several smaller parks provide welcome oases in the midst of the city's daily bustle—places like Union Square, Portsmouth Square, Mission Dolores, Buena Vista Park, Civic Center Plaza, Balboa Park, Baker's Beach, James D. Phelan State Beach, and Sigmund Stern Grove (adjacent to Pine Lake Park) where the firs, redwoods and eucalyptus trees form a natural setting for pop concerts, operettas, and Broadway musicals.

Golden Gate Bridge

Overleaf: From Twin Peaks, the city's geographic center, a marvelous view of downtown San Francisco along Market Street and the Oakland Bay Bridge

Left: The City and its famous Bridge

Left: The world-famous "Turn Around"—the Cable Car Turntable at Powell and Market Streets

The horse-drawn cars of the past provided at best a difficult mode of travel up San Francisco's steep hills. In 1863, cable cars were introduced to replace the old fashioned system, and this made it possible for the city's barons of industry to move up into the desirable Nob Hill section. Although only 17 miles of the original 112 miles of the system that crossed the city in 1880 remain, San Francisco today is the only city in the world to have an operating cable car system. The 39 cars have been known to transport as many as 25,000 people a day during the tourist season. Called "single-enders," the two Powell Street routes end at turntables where part of the fun is to help turn them around again.

A Cable Car and one of the numerous Flower Stands make a colorful combination.

A Cable Car climbing Hyde Street Hill.
In the Bay sits the island of Alcatraz.

Cable Car at Powell and Market Sts.

Overleaf: Bay Bridge at sundown.

The popular Fisherman's Wharf at night

Ghirardelli Square in a subdued mood

Fisherman's Wharf

The famous (infamous in the old days) Cliff House
on the western coast of the city, provides an
excellent view of the Pacific and
the Seal Rocks

San Francisco's Pier 39, next to Fisherman's Wharf

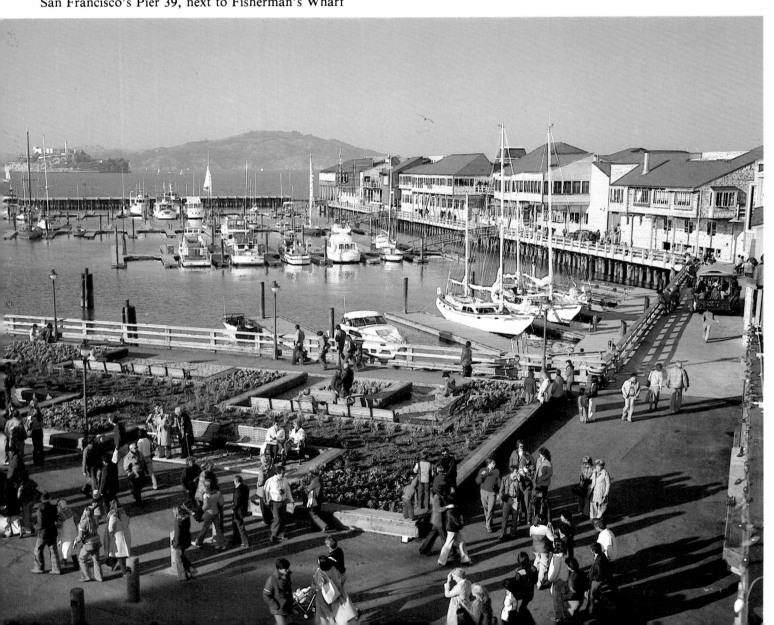

Preceding page:
Fishing fleet at
Fisherman's Wharf

Left: The financial district,
with the Transamerica
Building Pyramid and the
Bank of America Building
accenting the skyline

Right: The Cow Palace,
the home of the Annual
Grand National Livestock
Expositions. Many sports
programs and exhibitions
are held in the huge
auditorium.

Below: Street merchants
around the Hyde Street
Turntable

Lombard Street

"The crookedest street in the world."

San Francisco's graceful City Hall

St. Mary's Cathedral

St. Francis Hotel

One of the busy city's many oases is Union Square

Cable Car climbing down San Francisco Hill.

The Palace of Fine Arts, with its Greco-Romanesque rotunda and
Corinthian colonnades, graces the swan-filled lagoon. Built in 1915
for the Panama-Pacific Exposition, it was restored to its original
splendor in 1967. Now it is the home of the Exploratorium of science,
technology,and human perception.

Charming entrances to Victorian town houses

An aerial view of Sausalito—a Mediterranean style
community which has earned the reputation for being
especially hospitable to people interested in the arts.

Above: The University of California at Berkeley

Left: Two views of Stanford University.

Giant Redwoods in Marin County, across the Golden Gate Bridge from the city of San Francisco. These magnificent trees, many of them more than 200 feet in height and over 2,000 years old, occupy the Muir Woods, an area of 425 acres. They are among the world's oldest and tallest living things.

From The Beginnings

The name "Golden Gate" was not created in conjunction with the building of the world-famous bridge. Rather, the bridge took its name from the strait itself, that gap in the line of mountains that defines the shoreline of upper California. Captain John Charles Fremont (President Polk's Pathfinder), who had pushed westward overland with his scout Kit Carson, gave the strait its name in 1846, long before the bridge was even imagined.

How the mountain wall was breached by nature and the bay itself formed is still something of a mystery despite various theories about it. The Indian inhabitants believed that the strait had been formed by an ancient earthquake that had split the mountains and allowed the ocean to rush into the waiting inner valley, turning it into a bay.

The mystery of the gate's origin is compounded by the fact that several competent explorers, including Sir Francis Drake, had investigated this portion of the California coast during the sixteenth and seventeenth centuries, had even anchored at Point Reyes (some 30 miles to the northwest), without detecting the presence of the entrance to the exceptional bay. There's an irony here, since the purpose of those explorations was to find a suitable harbor on the northern coast of California.

One recent theory maintains that the strait was formed by waters of several rivers forcing their way through the developing mountains to the Pacific. Geologists believe that San Francisco Bay assumed its present formation twelve to fifteen thousand years ago, at the close of the Ice Age, when the melting ice caused the sea level to rise and flood the strait, filling the inner valley.

This doesn't explain the explorers' failure to discover the Gate, of course. One of the reasons offered for this failure is that the strait was most likely hidden by fog. This may have been the case in the summer months, but in the winter the fog forms inland and is fairly thinned by the time it reaches the coastal areas. And there were explorers who did sail the coast in the winter months (Carmeno in 1595 and Vizcaino in 1604) without detecting the strait.

The bay was discovered by the white man in 1769. A land expedition, led by Gaspar de Portola, had worked its way northward along the coast from San Diego and had missed its intended goal, Monterey Bay. The tired men climbed over Montara Mountain (in the present San Mateo area) and camped at its northern base. Don Portola, next day, sent a group of men to explore the coast farther north, and this party discovered the strait.

Other Spaniards investigated the newfound harbor during the next several years. The first ship to actually sail into the strait was the *San Carlos,* commanded by Juan Manuel de Ayala. The strong tides made the initial anchorage points near the Gate unsafe, and Ayala spent whole month conducting extensive explorations in the harbor after establishing an anchorage in a sheltered cove of the bay's largest island. He named this island *Isla de Nuestra Senora do Los Angeles* ("Isle of Our Lady of the Angels" or, as we know it, Angel Island.)

The first white settlements, established in 1776, were the Presidio and the Mission San Francisco de Assisi (Mission Dolores). The Presidio ("military post" or "fort") was built near the southern jaw of the Gate and afforded an excellent view of the strait, the headlands across the water gap, and Point Reyes.

In 1776, Captain Juan Batista de Anza led an expedition of soldiers and colonists from Sonora in northern Mexico to Monterey, which was a Mexican outpost at the time. With a smaller group, Anza proceeded farther up the coast, camping on the shores of Mountain Lake (which would become a water supply for the Presidio, and later for San Francisco). With six men, Anza scouted westward to Point Lobos. It was decided that the Presidio would be erected on a mesa near the Point.

The Mission San Francisco de Assisi was established by the priest Junipero Serra that same year. The name Dolores was taken from nearby *Laguna de Nuestra Senora de los Dolores* ("Lake of Our Lady of Sorrows") which was later filled in.

These first settlements were largely ignored by Mexico and did not flourish. One other area was colonized in 1835-36, a small settlement southeast of Telegraph Hill. It was given the name *Yerba Buena* ("Good Herb") because of the rambling wild mint that spread over the land. *Yerba Buena* was the bud that flowered later into San Francisco. For a time, all three settlements were referred to as *Yerba Buena*. During its 70 years of static existence, the small population, mostly military, subsisted on trade in pelts and tallow. But by the beginning of the nineteenth century, *Yerba Buena* had become a favorite stopping place for sea captains from New England, Britain, and Russia.

The topography did not encourage development of the area. The hills were steep and barren, and they rose amid shifting sand dunes. The eastern part of the peninsula was somewhat more accommodating; the land sloped gently to the bay. In the late 1830s, "San Francisco" was being used to designate the settlement around Mission Dolores, the Presidio installation, and the new *Yerba Buena*. As the latter developed, the other two settlements waned. The first real house in the San Francisco area was built at *Yerba Buena* by an Englishman, Captain William A. Richardson in 1835, and in 1836 the first store was erected nearby.

To Captain John Charles Fremont goes the credit for quietly bringing about the revolt of a group of Americans at Sonoma. The Spanish dream had been to extend New Spain from Mexico up into the western coast of the northern hemisphere. But Spain ceded California to Mexico in 1822, so the San Francisco area fell under Mexican rule. In 1846, the Sonoma revolt took place, and a few days later, Captain James Montgomery and a group of marines from the *USS Portsmouth,* which was anchored in Yerba Buena Cove, marched up the slope to what is now Portsmouth Square and planted the American flag. In 1847, the pueblo of *Yerba Buena* was officially renamed "San Francisco."

In January of the same year, Sam Brannan, the Mormon leader, had begun publishing California's first newspaper—the weekly *California Star.* The *Californian* appeared in May.

By 1848, the city's population was between 800 and 900. But on January 24, 1848, gold was discovered by James Marshall at John Sutter's sawmill. San Francisco became a ghost town temporarily as every able-bodied man dashed off to look for gold. Soon afterward, however, San Francisco became the center of a booming business in miner's supplies, bawdy entertainment, and gold exchange. When the news of the gold strike finally reached the East, San Francisco's population increased to a phenomenal 25,000 in less than two years. Goods became scarce, and demand was so great that apples were selling for $5 each and the going price for eggs was $1 apiece. Shipping traffic in the bay went up dramatically. In 1849 alone, 549 ships dropped anchor inside the Golden Gate. The Exchange and Deposits Office (San Francisco's first commercial bank) opened on Kearny Street.

At midcentury, San Francisco was incorporated as a city, and California was admitted to the Union. By the close of 1851, more than 25,000 emigrants had passed through the Gate. The influx started in 1850 with a fleet of 40 vessels carrying 1,000 Chinese people to the new land.

The infamous Barbary Coast flourished in the early 1850s. Shanghaiing, getting men drunk, kidnapping them, and selling them to waiting sea captains who needed to fill out their crews, was a lucrative venture and went unchecked. Aided by corrupt government officials, crime reached such proportions that a second Vigilance Committee had to be formed. It wasn't until 1904 that Congress passed a law prohibiting shanghaiing in the United States.

The first Vigilance Committee had been formed in 1851 under the leadership of Sam Brannan. After a few wrongdoers were hanged by the Committee, several of the worst criminals wisely decided to leave town.

The year 1856 marked the beginnings of political reform, but criminal activities and problems continued to exist.

Since San Francisco had been taken from the Mexicans by a "military action" in 1846, a tug-of-war had continued between the military and civilian factions as to who should rule and control the city. By the end of 1848, things became so confused that there were in existence at the same time one military and three civil governments of San Francisco. Finally, in June 1849, when the Convention was called to frame the State Constitution, the competing groups became reconciled, and the city came under unified civilian control.

The first public school in San Francisco was established in 1849 also. Four years later, California's first telegraph line was strung from Point Lobos to Telegraph Hill.

Dueling as an "honorable" way of settling disputes reached its height in the mid-1850s. The last duel in San Francisco was fought between U.S. Senator David C. Broderick and State Supreme Court Chief Justice David S. Terry. Broderick died as a result of the wounds he received in the exchange.

To add to the excitement occasioned by the 1848 gold strike, silver was discovered in the Sierra Nevada in 1859, and many San Franciscans rushed to the mountains to establish or renew their fortunes. San Francisco's economy, which had begun to sag, was revived instantly, and from 1859 to 1877, the "silver era" involved the city in another sustained economic boom.

The year 1860 marked the introduction of mail delivery between the West Coast port and the East—by pony express at a cost of $5 per half ounce of mail.

When the Civil War broke out, California experienced some heated debates but finally decided to stay with the Union. While the economy continued to expand, vast fortunes were being made in silver ore and growing railroads. Snobbish rivalry was responsible for the construction of ornate mansions and palaces on Nob Hill as the industrial barons struggled to outdo each other—to the extent of importing materials from foreign lands, including marble all the way from China. The San Francisco Stock Exchange opened in 1862. In 1869, the Central Pacific Railroad reached Oakland. In 1917, state and city laws finally shut down the notorious Barbary Coast.

The opening of the Panama Canal in 1851 gave a welcome boost to San Francisco's shipping trade. San Franciscans saw the canal as a sign that the future of their city was assured. And the Panama-Pacific International Exposition, celebrating the canal opening for almost the entire year, confirmed this confidence in the city's health and growth. San Franciscans realized anew their ability to participate in international and world-wide events, whatever problems they might be having at home. One of the buildings from that Exposition, the Palace of Fine Arts designed by Bernard Maybeck, would remain as a landmark in the city, and would be rebuilt in the 1960s.

In 1945, the beginning steps to the formation of the United Nations took place in San Francisco. Delegates from fifty countries attended the United Nations Conference on International Organization and signed the United Nations Charter on June 26 of that year.

Historic Telegraph Hill   Victorian Houses.

The Fateful Year—1906

On the morning of April 18, at 12 minutes 6 seconds after 5 o'clock, while the people of San Francisco still slept, the San Andreas fault settled. The earthquake ended at 13 minutes 11 seconds after 5, but that minute and five seconds proved very costly to the city of San Francisco. the fires resulting from the quake wiped out four square miles of the business sector. An area of about 500 city blocks (30,000 buildings) was destroyed. The known dead totaled 500.

Heavy damage occurred along the California coast, from the southern part of Fresno County up to Humboldt County. But earthquake damage to San Francisco itself was light compared to the havoc wreaked by the fires. While firefighters and volunteers fought the flames with unstinting courage, half the city's population were forced to spend several nights outdoors. About 200,000 camped on the grounds of the Golden Gate Park. Space in the Presidio Military Reservation accommodated another 50,000.

Fires had been the bane of the young city's life. In 1849, the first in a series of disastrous blazes burned down some 50 houses valued at $1,250,000. In May of 1851, a fire destroyed the business sector, and a month later another fire leveled 16 blocks. Cisterns were constructed under the streets in 1852 to store water for emergencies. These were to prove of use in 1906, when the earthquake broke the water mains.

Earthquakes too were nothing new to San Franciscans. Tremors and light shocks were a common occurrence and attracted little attention. Four of the previous shocks were described as "exceptionally severe," and three other (1830, 1865, 1868) were actually classified "destructive." The worst of these, the one in 1868, cracked a few aging buildings and caused five deaths.

But the series of shocks that struck the city on the morning of April 18 and the fires that raged out of control for three days, along with some lesser aftershocks, demolished the entire business section and adjoining areas.

The broken water mains made matters worse. The underground cisterns helped in fighting the fires, but they lacked the pressure the mains would have provided. The weary firefighters dynamited rows of buildings in an effort to confine the fires within one major area. Many elaborate mansions on Van Ness Avenue were sacrificed.

The fires were finally checked at Franklin Street. The city was placed under military control because of the extent of the damage, and the troops aided in the work of relief and salvage. On April 21, it was reported that the fires had been brought under control. The huge task of rebuilding the city and rehabilitating the citizens got under way. The value of the destroyed buildings was assessed at about $105,000,000, but the total loss in damage to property was presumed to be between $350,000,000 and $500,000,000.

As soon as the ashes had cooled enough, the people entered the area and began picking up the pieces. By April 26 (five days after the fires had been checked and only eight days after the initial quake), merchants reopened their fire-scarred doors and offered tremendous sales. Reconstruction began. New power lines were installed in a matter of days. The wrecked sewers were repaired. Wider streets were planned.

Financial assistance arrived from diverse sources, from Europe and Asia as well as from the money centers of the East Coast. In three years, a new San Francisco stood on the site of the old, a truly heroic accomplishment.

The determination and speed with which the city recovered from the worst disaster in its history illustrates clearly the character and indomitable spirit of the people of San Francisco.

The China Gate
the entrance to Chinatown at
Grant Avenue and Bush Street

Cities Within, A City

From the heart of the city where it starts to its end in an abrupt descent to the Bay, Grant Avenue is only about a mile and a half long. But it is the most varied mile and a half imaginable. In a few hours, you can walk through several of San Francisco's worlds—an area of sophisticated shops, Chinatown's chief thoroughfare, the Bohemian Broadway, and a neighborhood of old Italian homes, stores, and pasta factories.

Not that all the different cultures are found in the Grant Avenue area, however. Other colonies are scattered throughout the city, in the Mission district, the Western Addition, the Richmond district, and on Potrero Hill. This composition of diverse cultures adds to San Francisco's personality. About 60 different national groups co-exist in the city. Church services are offered regularly in 23 languages. There are 25 newspapers published in 14 languages, including Italian, Chinese, Japanese, and Russian daily editions.

The various groups celebrate their national and traditional holidays, giving the city a continual air of festivity. The Scots have their Robert Burns Day, The Welsh celebrate St. David's Day in their ancient Cymric tongue, and the Greeks observe their Independence Day. The Poles remember Pulaski Day, and the Italians celebrate Columbus Day. The Chinese and Japanese observe their rituals and holidays, too, and San Francisco seems always about to break into a brisk folk dance or to begin a parade.

Chinatown This includes an area of Grant Avenue from Bush Street to Columbus Avenue and the side streets branching off the Avenue. Passing through the China Gate at Grant Avenue and Bush Street, one enters the largest Chinese community outside the Orient. More than fifty percent of the Chinese in San Francisco are American born. Older men and women in traditional clothing mix with younger Chinese in Western garb.

On Waverly Place, west of Grant Avenue at Clay Street, is the fourth floor site of *Tien Hou* (Temple to the Queen of Heaven) which was dedicated in 1852 as a token of gratitude for the safe arrival of Chinese immigrants to San Francisco. Buddha's Universal Church, the largest Buddist church in this country, faces Portsmouth Square. The Chinese Historical Society of America is located on Adler Place, off Grant Avenue between Pacific Avenue and Broadway. The only authentic Chinese Wax Museum in America is located on Grant Avenue at California Street.

Iron-grilled balconies and pagoda roofs line the area. Restaurants feature the various Chinese cuisines. Shops and bazaars offer silks, jewelry, porcelain and lacquered objects of every description. Joss-houses (temples) in which the Chinese worship as their ancestors have for hundreds of generations are located throughout Chinatown. The eye is attracted to the exotic architecture of the buildings, shop windows displaying Buddha statues, jade objects, abacuses of various sizes, designs, and materials, colorfully decorated screens, scrolls, teakwood furniture, and ornately carved tables and chests. Women in beautifully tailored Oriental dresses shop at the open markets for the chicken or duck they will serve for the evening meal. During daylight hours, the streets are crowded mostly with the inhabitants of the area. It appears to be a congested scene, but things proceed in an amazingly ordered fashion. In the evening and night hours, tourists throng Chinatown, increasing the bustle of the streets. They are looking for some trace of the earlier Chinatown but are caught up in the contemporary one by the sheer beauty of the lights etching the lines of the Oriental buildings. Most corners of Chinatown display at open stands huge jars of pistachio nuts and lichee nuts, ginger coconut, candied melon, along with penny candy and chewing gum. Store windows are filled with Oriental cooking utensils.

On Pine Street (off Grant Avenue) is the Kong Chow Temple, a brick structure with a tiled roof and pagoda style architecture. The temple was dedicated in 1857 to Kwan Ti, a general who lived around 400B.C. and is a symbol of courage. The original temple was destroyed by fire in the 1906 disaster, but the statue of Kwan Ti survived the flames and a new shrine was built at the Pine Street location. Across the street in St. Mary's Square stands a statue honoring Sun Yat-sen, the father of modern China. Sculptor Beniamino Bufano used rose-colored granite for the face and hands, and the figure is draped in stainless steel robes. Sun Yat-sen came often to San Francisco's Chinatown to raise money for the 1911 revolution in China. It is said that he plotted the course of the revolution against the Manchu dynasty from an office in the old Montgomery Block.

The first Chinese came to this country during the time of the gold rush. They demonstrated a conscientious application and a manual dexterity that won them the reputation of being good workers. Later, they were imported by the thousands to work on the extending railroads across the Sierra Nevada Mountains. When that work was completed, they returned to San Francisco, increasing the already sizeable Chinese population in the city substantially. They became mechanics, cigarmakers, shoemakers, and fishermen.

When hard times came to the new city, the Chinese did not fare well. They were forced to create their own world, and that world has maintained its individuality up to this day.

On Stockton Street, one block west of Grant Avenue, is a building with a blue, glazed surface, a red-tiled roof, and balconies projecting from the front wall. This is the headquarters of the Six Companies. The Six Companies is an association formed by the first Chinese who came to the Bay City and is modeled after the relationships of the districts in Kangtung Province where they were born. This organization and others like it actually govern Chinatown, creating a city within the city.

Of San Francisco's estimated 38,000 Chinese, more than 20,000 of them live in the Chinese district known as Chinatown. It is a crowded area, but most of the people prefer to live in an area that resembles their homeland as closely as possible.

One of the most exciting and decorative events in Chinatown is the celebration of the Chinese New Year, a week of festivities coming between mid-January and late February, depending on the fullness of the moon. The streets are lined with flower stands, the shrines are exquisitely decorated, and a good brotherly feeling permeates the district. The parades feature bands of all nationalities, and a papier-mache lion prances bravely ahead of the musicians.

But the festive spirit persists all year 'round. The dragon-entwined lampposts and incense-filled air make one feel he is truly in an exotic country.

North Beach Grant Avenue from Columbus Avenue branches out into the section known as North Beach. Besides being the heart of the Italian settlement, North Beach is also the focal point of San Francisco's night life and the locale of the city's Bohemian colony. Up the slopes of Telegraph Hill nestles an expensive residential area.

Coffee houses abound, and every form of entertainment imaginable can be found in North Beach's Broadway. Music from Gay Nineties tunes to the latest jazz styles may be heard here. And here too will be found the best restaurants in the city. Columbus Avenue has a more subdued air, more conservative night clubs and restaurants, and is primarily the main street of the Italian neighborhood. Closer to Telegraph Hill, as the streets incline more steeply, one can sense what the area was like in earlier years when the first Bohemians lived side by side with the Italians of the time. It is a quieter area, watched over by the Coit Tower on the top of the hill and pedestaled by the docks and ships below.

More than 68,000 San Franciscans are Italian or of Italian ancestry, forming the largest national group in the city. And most of them live in the Columbus Avenue area.

In the middle of the last century, before San Francisco became a city, there were very few Italians residing in San Francisco. Within the last half of the 1800s, Italian fishermen began to arrive in their fishing boats. Before the century reached its close, they had formed a sizeable component of the city's population. Most of them settled in the North Beach section.

The center of this Italian town within the city is Washington Square, at the intersection of Columbus Avenue and Union Street. The major event of the year is the Columbus Day parade, with floats symbolizing the voyage of the Genoese sailor and with bands playing marches and mazurkas familiar to every resident. Thousands of Italians participate in the festivities. The parade starts at the Church of St. Peter and St. Paul of the fishing fleet. The celebration includes a champagne Coronation Ball at the Italian Consulate-General. Another parade makes its way from Market Street to North Beach. When the landing of Christopher Columbus is reenacted in Aquatic Park, the Coast Guard is on hand to assist in the landing.

San Francisco Italians have held on to their identity in spite of encroachments on their area from time to time—especially by Bohemians and beatniks. Something about San Francisco makes the Italian residents feel as if they are in their own Italy. They love it, and most of them wouldn't leave it for any other place in the world.

Japantown "Nihonmachi" is the name the more than 12,000 Japanese San Franciscans have for the district known as Japantown. The area includes the new, lavishly conceived and constructed Japan Center, an assortment of showrooms, shops, coffee and tea houses, a tempura bar, a theatre, a hotel, and the Peace Plaza. The Peace Plaza is topped by a five-tier pagoda. In the Plaza are held the Spring Cherry Blossom Festival and the annual Fall Festival. Japan Center provides the Japanese community with a central location where the people can observe their traditional holidays and customs. It is also a profitable commercial venture.

Japantown is located in the Western Addition, around Post and Buchanan Streets. There are several small but fine restaurants in the area, and the food they serve is simple and wholesome. Japanese movies are shown on weekend evenings at Kimnon Hall, often films about the famed Samurai warriors.

The Japanese community was uprooted during World War II, but the Japanese Americans have reestablished their community with great success.

At the Japanese-Bonn Festival every August, it is not unusual to see Americanized Nisei join their more traditional brethren in the ritual dances as the older Japanese honor the dead with offerings in the temples.

Text continued on page 70.

Chinatown Streets

North Beach

Above: The Japanese Cultural and Trade Center

Below: The Japanese Tea Garden in the Golden Gate Park

Bohemia Not long ago, a few artists and Bohemians lived quietly with their Italian neighbors on the slopes of Telegraph Hill and along upper Grant Avenue. then came the beatniks who established themselves and made the area temporarily their own. This attracted tourists which in turn attracted smart business people ready to exploit the situation. Young men and women sporting the symbolic clothing and jewelry of the beatniks may still be seen on the streets, but their influence has all but disappeared, and the district is returning to its old, more sedate character.

The first Bohemian in San Francisco was probably Cincinnatus Heine Miller, in the 1870s. He didn't care much for his name so he changed it to Joaquin Miller (after the Mexican "Robin Hood"—Joaquin Murieta, whom he greatly admired).

The San Francisco Bohemian Club was formed by a group of writers, artists, and newspapermen who decided to meet once a month to discuss art. Their discussions were frequently accompanied by generous portions of liquid refreshments, and the meetings were quite lively. Today, the Bohemian Club occupies a 2,500-acre redwood grove on the Russian River and is one of San Francisco's most exclusive clubs. Its present respectability is in direct contrast with its early romps when the club's meeting place was a few tables and chairs in an otherwise empty room.

From time to time, other Bohemian colonies have settled in San Francisco—on Telegraph Hill, on Russian Hill, and more recently on Potrero Hill.

There are other national communities in San Francisco. The Russians have settled on Potrero Hill. The Irish were clustered in the Mission district but have since merged with all parts of the city. And the Filipinos occupy an area on the edges of Chinatown and North Beach, along Kearny Street.

Out of all these settlements and colonies comes the population profile of San Francisco. It is a melding without blurring the identities of the individual groups. The result is a congregation of cultures perhaps unlike that of any other American city.

All San Franciscans are proud of their city and will happily play the role of press agent in boosting it. But within the city, most people keep their distinctive heritage, for they must realize at some deep level if they surrender totally to the melting pot, San Francisco risks losing one of those special qualities that make it unique.

San Francisco is a city easy to love. And it's true, as the song says, that San Francisco will steal your heart. Having once experienced San Francisco, one can never forget the City by the Golden Gate.

Right: Coit Tower on top of Telegraph Hill.

San Francisco—the old, young city.